St. Joan of Arc

SAINTS
YOU SHOULD KNOW SERIES

St. Joan of Arc

Margaret and
Matthew Bunson

Our Sunday Visitor Publishing Division
Our Sunday Visitor, Inc.
Huntington, Indiana 46750

ISBN: 0-87973-784-0 (hardcover)
ISBN: 0-87973-558-9 (softcover)
LCCCN: 91-68359

PRINTED IN THE UNITED STATES OF AMERICA

Cover and text illustrations by Margaret Bunson

Foreword

St. Joan of Arc, one of the most popular saints in the modern world, is a mysterious sort of historical figure. She came out of "nowhere" to save her king and to help shape the nation of France. Caught in the terrible tragedy of the Hundred Years War, Joan died at the hands of her enemies because she would not deny the fact that God had sent her to perform such tasks.

Joan was courageous, daring, and — quite surprisingly — a military tactician, which is a fancy way of saying that she knew how to send the English armies running in panic. Her letters to the English commanders have survived, and they reveal a young woman with brains, determination, and honor. The fact that she was abandoned by the very king that she saved, even by her comrades-in-arms, did not stop Joan from obeying what she knew to be the will of God. Her death at the fiery stake was not only cruel and needless but crowned her purity and her loyalty to her mission.

Few of us will be visited by angels and saints and asked to save our nation and our nation's leader. The days of armies and Crusades have paled, but there are wrongs to be righted, injustices to correct, and people who need care and understanding. Our age needs as much courage, as much daring and loyalty to the will of God, as the age of Joan. Her message remains as everlasting and enduring.

MARGARET AND MATTHEW BUNSON

Pronunciation Guide

Alençon (all-on-sewn)

Anjou (on-zhoo)

Augustines (oh-goos-teen)

Auxerre (ohz-air)

bastilles (bass-tee-yuh)

Baudricourt (boh-dri-coor)

Bourbonnais (boor-bon-ay)

Bourges (boor-zhuh)

Bouvreuil (boo-vrew-eel)

Brehal (bray-al)

Burey (bure-ay)

Catherine de Fierbois, Ste.
    (sant-cat-air-een-duh-fee-air-bwa)

Cauchon, Pierre (pee-air coh-shown)

Ceffonds (seff-owned)

Chinon (sheen-own)

Compiègne (cohm-pee-en-yuh)

dauphin (doh-fan)

Denis, St. (san-day-nee)

d'Estouteville (det-oot-veal)

Digne (deen-yuh)

Domrémy (dohm-ray-mee)

Du Lys (due-lee)

Dunois (dune-wa)

Étienne de Vignoles
    (ate-ee-en-duh-veen-yohl)

Florentine, St. (san-flor-on-teen)

Foix (fwa)

Hauves de Poulvoir
    (hoe-vuh-duh-pool-vwar)

Hire, La (la-ear)

Jargeau (zhar-go)

Jean le Blanc, St. (san-zhon-luh-blonk)

Laxart, Durand (due-ron-laz-ar)

Loup, St. (san-loo)

Metz, Jean de (zhon-duh-mets)

Meuse (moohz)

Midi, Nicholas (nee-ko-la-mee-dee)

Moselle (moh-zell)

Neant (nay-on)

Neufchâteau (noof-shah-toh)

Orléans (or-lay-on)

Place du Vieux-Marché
    (plos-due-vyuwh-mar-
    shay)

Poitou (pwa-too)

Poucelle, La (la-poo-sell)

Pouligny, Bertrand de
    (bair-tron-duh-pool-
    ee-nyee)

Reims (rem)

Rouen (roo-on)

Tourelles (toor-el)

Tours (toor)

Troyes (troy)

Valois (val-wa)

Vouthon (voo-tone)

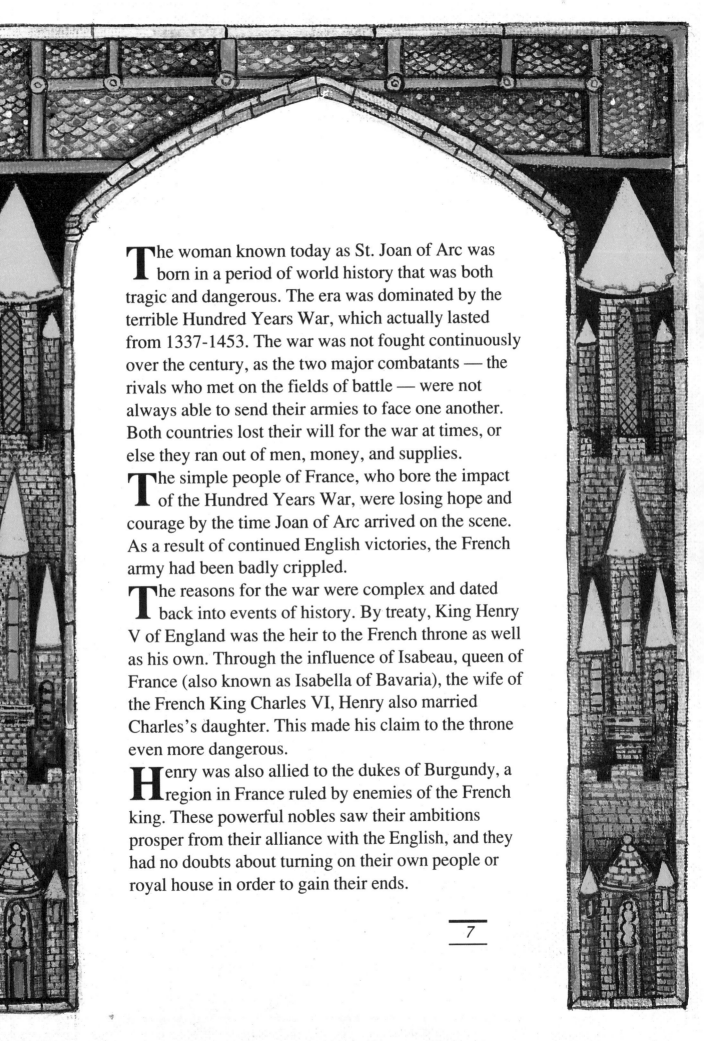

The woman known today as St. Joan of Arc was born in a period of world history that was both tragic and dangerous. The era was dominated by the terrible Hundred Years War, which actually lasted from 1337-1453. The war was not fought continuously over the century, as the two major combatants — the rivals who met on the fields of battle — were not always able to send their armies to face one another. Both countries lost their will for the war at times, or else they ran out of men, money, and supplies.

The simple people of France, who bore the impact of the Hundred Years War, were losing hope and courage by the time Joan of Arc arrived on the scene. As a result of continued English victories, the French army had been badly crippled.

The reasons for the war were complex and dated back into events of history. By treaty, King Henry V of England was the heir to the French throne as well as his own. Through the influence of Isabeau, queen of France (also known as Isabella of Bavaria), the wife of the French King Charles VI, Henry also married Charles's daughter. This made his claim to the throne even more dangerous.

Henry was also allied to the dukes of Burgundy, a region in France ruled by enemies of the French king. These powerful nobles saw their ambitions prosper from their alliance with the English, and they had no doubts about turning on their own people or royal house in order to gain their ends.

The dauphin, the son of King Charles VI and known in time as Charles VII, was called the dauphin because of the lands that he ruled in his right. Raised a royal prince, he was in a sorry state when his father died in 1422. He could not hope to be crowned the rightful king because the coronation had to take place in the city of Reims. The English had taken Reims during the war, and they expected that their own monarch, Henry V, would take the crown as his own. The dauphin was only the king of the Bourges because that was the only city in which the people accepted his claims to the throne and honored him.

France was not much of a country at the time, of course, being splintered into a number of small kingdoms or petty states. The nobles of these realms — an old word for kingdom — fought for power, snubbed the king, and generally made life miserable for one another. Orléans, Anjou, Foix, Bourbonnais, Poitou, and Burgundy, as well as a group of still smaller realms, watched the outcomes of the battles and sided with the winners of the time.

The Burgundians especially wanted Charles VII, the dauphin, either dead or tightly locked into his own small territory. The dauphin, realizing this, felt that he had no prospects of winning the war and not even a remote chance of being crowned. He was also a man without drive, a man who allowed his advisers to run his life and to plot against each other. The dauphin was considered dim-witted, perhaps even an imbecile, by many in France and England at the time.

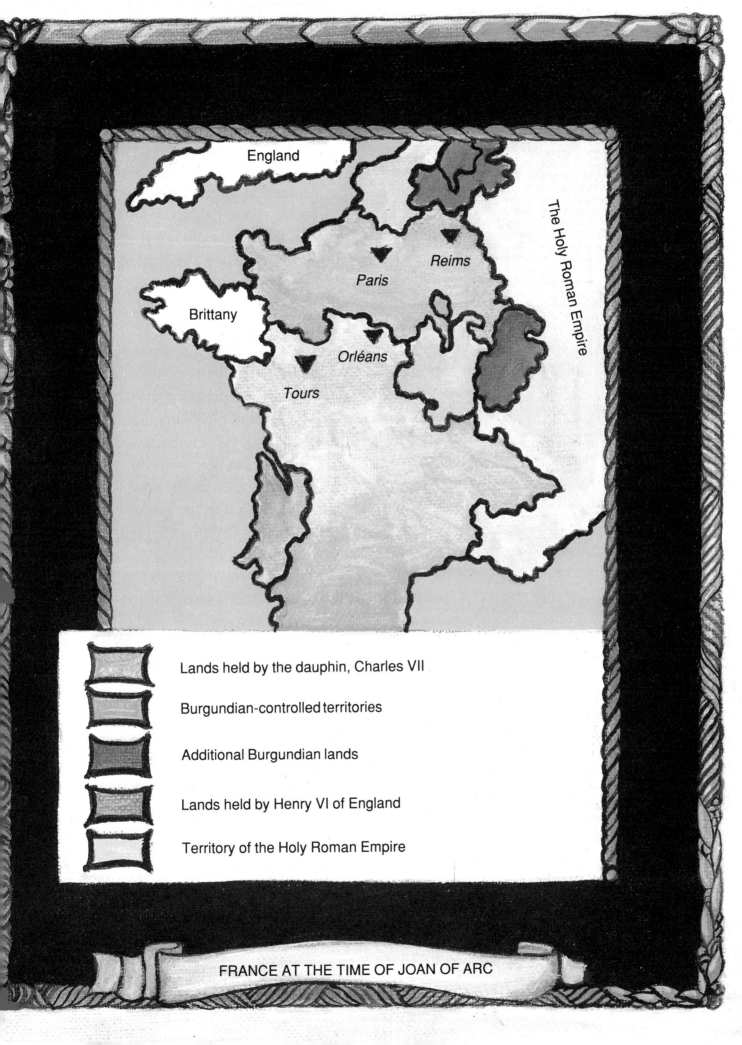

FRANCE AT THE TIME OF JOAN OF ARC

The French people, those who lived in the villages or on the farms, suffered terribly because of the war between France and England and because of the treacherous ambitions of the French noble houses. Raids against various regions were constantly conducted by mercenaries — grim, ferocious warriors who were paid to fight — and they burned down villages and looted when they did not receive their wages. They killed the farmers and townspeople and carried off everything they could lay their hands on in their raids. As a result, stalking across the countryside behind the mercenaries came starvation, plague, and the terrible winter cold.

Throughout all of the death and destruction, the people prayed as they saw their nation lay in broken pieces. They hoped for peace across all of France, and they begged God to send them a champion who would stir the hearts of their countrymen and their king. Most of the French blamed Queen Isabeau, the mother of the dauphin, who had forced her royal husband to make Henry V his heir. Isabeau, mother and queen, had started France on the road to ruin. A prophecy making the rounds in the country said that a virgin woman would rise up to save the land in time of need.

The French people did not know that this virgin woman was already alive and waiting for the sign to move against the nation's enemies.

10

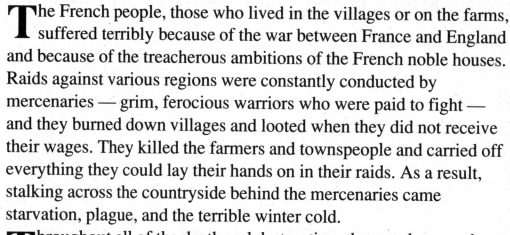

QUEEN ISABEAU

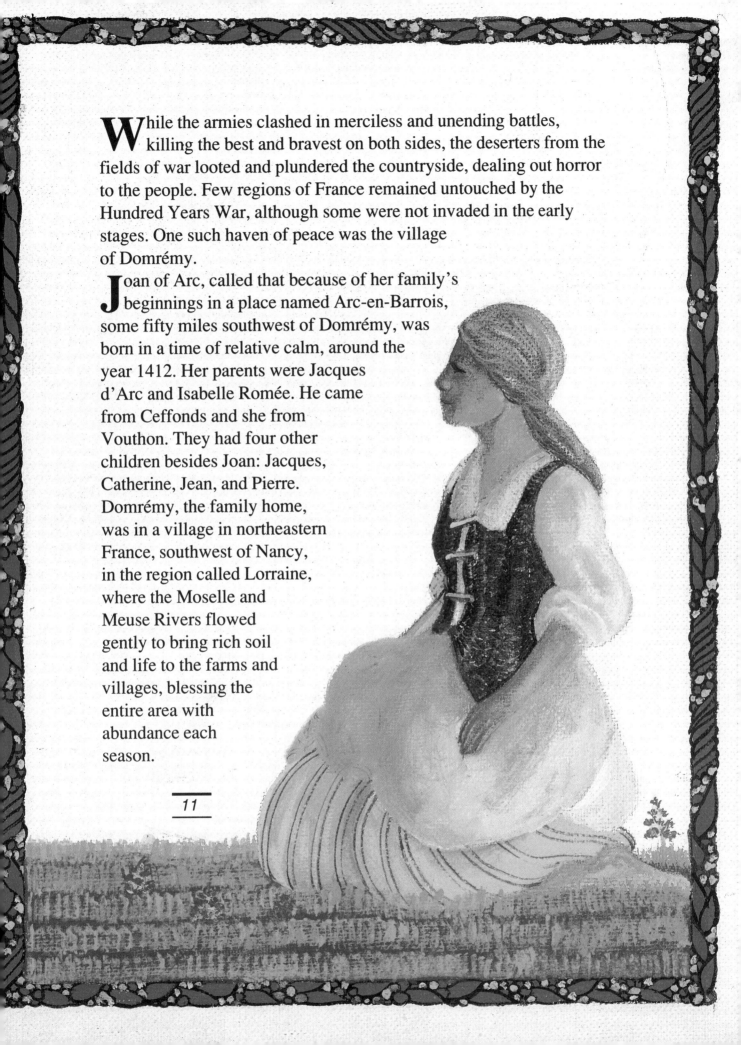

While the armies clashed in merciless and unending battles, killing the best and bravest on both sides, the deserters from the fields of war looted and plundered the countryside, dealing out horror to the people. Few regions of France remained untouched by the Hundred Years War, although some were not invaded in the early stages. One such haven of peace was the village of Domrémy.

Joan of Arc, called that because of her family's beginnings in a place named Arc-en-Barrois, some fifty miles southwest of Domrémy, was born in a time of relative calm, around the year 1412. Her parents were Jacques d'Arc and Isabelle Romée. He came from Ceffonds and she from Vouthon. They had four other children besides Joan: Jacques, Catherine, Jean, and Pierre. Domrémy, the family home, was in a village in northeastern France, southwest of Nancy, in the region called Lorraine, where the Moselle and Meuse Rivers flowed gently to bring rich soil and life to the farms and villages, blessing the entire area with abundance each season.

DOMRÉMY

There have been many attempts over the years to link Joan of Arc to the royal family, perhaps to explain her actions and her ability to lead people of all classes into battle. Her direct ties with the royal House of Valois have never been proven. Her father, Jacques d'Arc, was certainly not a nobleman. He kept sheep, farmed a few acres of land, and enjoyed the goodwill of his neighbors, who elected him to public office. The household was typical of the time: pious, thrifty, and loving. Rooted in the soil and to the great turning cycle of seasons, the family worked hard and understood the value of prayer and personal virtues. Joan and her brothers and sister, probably learned their prayers from their mother at an early age.

Their lives were normal, part of a rural community, where life and chores depended upon the weather, the changes in the sky and fields, and on the liturgical cycles of the Church. Joan performed small chores around the house and then became a shepherdess. Early on, however, she did show an unusual liking for the sound of bells. Such bells, echoing over the countryside, would have called the people to the ancient prayer called the Angelus. Joan paid the local sexton — the caretaker of the parish church — in wool and cakes, just to make sure that he rang the bells properly.

She prayed often, at times staying apart from other youngsters her age, but she was not considered odd by the townspeople. The entire community would have viewed her with alarm had they known about her personal life, and Joan was wise enough to keep it secret. She was hearing voices. These were not the ravings of poltergeists (that is, ghosts), and she did not imagine the messages that she received from them. She first heard the voices in 1425, a few months after the village heard about a great English victory at the battle of Veneuil on August 17, 1424. Such news would have taken months to travel to the remote parts of France.

The word, of course, depressed everyone because it meant that there was little hope of the dauphin chasing the hated English from the land. Now all of the local areas would be in danger. There were no mighty armies to stop the English advance.

13

Joan was looking toward the local church when she saw a light and heard the sound of a voice. She was frightened at first because she was sane enough to know that such things did not happen normally.

The voice, however, calmed her, told her to be a good girl, and that she would rescue the dauphin of France. The voice also spoke of the "pity that was the kingdom of France." Joan knew from the start that the voice talking to her was that of St. Michael the Archangel.

Being a practical young woman, she did not run screaming through the streets that voices were telling her the future. She also kept secret the vision that followed — that of St. Michael, in the company of other angels. St. Michael told her that she was to go "to France," which was a way of saying that she was to visit Paris, or the court of the king. The nation was in such a broken condition that many regions did not even consider themselves part of France itself. On her journey, Joan was told, she would be aided and comforted by St. Catherine and St. Margaret. They appeared to her on a later date, near a beautiful old tree, and whenever Joan went near the tree, the saints became visible again. Joan noticed the sweet smell of incense when the two saints were with her. She wept when they vanished, begging them to take her with them to heaven.

14

Staying on the farm with her family, Joan learned all of the household chores that were expected of women at the time. She avoided more and more the company of others her own age, those who spent their free hours dancing and telling stories. She did mention once to her mother that she would like to join the soldiers who fought for the dauphin. It may have been a test, to see what sort of reaction the family would have. Her father, upon hearing about her desire, said that he would drown her before he would allow his daughter to do such a mad thing.

In time, of course, even the sturdy farmers and villagers of the region of Lorraine saw their lands and their homes threatened. In July of 1428, Domrémy was attacked by a large group of Burgundians, now in total alliance with the English. Even the local church was robbed and burned, but the troops went away with little to show for their murderous efforts. The people of Domrémy, who had fled to the nearby fortified town of Neufchâteau, had few possessions and no wealth at all. While in the haven of Neufchâteau, Joan worked in a small inn. She returned with the other villagers and her family to Domrémy to see the destruction caused there.

The English and their allies were marching all across the land at will, threatening the Loire Valley and the city of Orléans, the last stronghold of the dauphin. France was in danger of falling into the hands of the English, and Charles VII, the rightful king, was being advised to seek safety in some other court of Europe.

THE DAUPHIN, CHARLES VII

Joan probably did not understand the many political and military strategies behind the news of the siege of Orléans, but she knew that the time had come for her to save the heir to the French throne. If he was a bit odd, given to laziness and inertia — remaining unmoved until he was pushed into doing something — that did not matter. The dauphin was France, and the voices told Joan to rise up in his defense.

She was told to go to Robert de Baudricourt, an official who would provide her with troops. Such a journey involved disobeying her parents, something that Joan had never done in her life. The voices and her visions, however, urged her to act courageously.

She decided not to tell her parents about her plans, and she turned to a relative, a man named Durand Laxart, of Burey, whom she called "Uncle." Joan asked him to gain her parents' permission for her to care for Durand's sick wife. He was happy to employ her in this service, and she left Domrémy with him. He believed that she was going to relieve him of a terrible burden in the care of his wife. Joan, however, knew that she had been asked by Almighty God to care for another critically wounded patient: the country of France. Her departure from Domrémy — marking the beginning of her public life — has been set as sometime in late December 1428. The prophecy was coming true. The virgin young woman had risen to defend the nation.

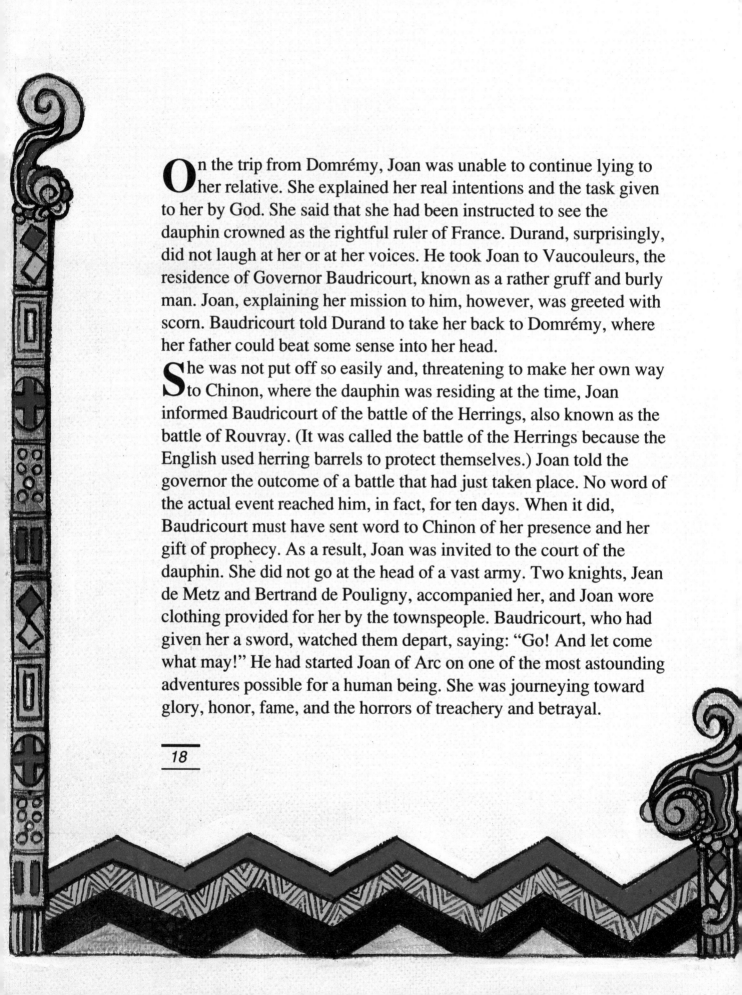

On the trip from Domrémy, Joan was unable to continue lying to her relative. She explained her real intentions and the task given to her by God. She said that she had been instructed to see the dauphin crowned as the rightful ruler of France. Durand, surprisingly, did not laugh at her or at her voices. He took Joan to Vaucouleurs, the residence of Governor Baudricourt, known as a rather gruff and burly man. Joan, explaining her mission to him, however, was greeted with scorn. Baudricourt told Durand to take her back to Domrémy, where her father could beat some sense into her head.

She was not put off so easily and, threatening to make her own way to Chinon, where the dauphin was residing at the time, Joan informed Baudricourt of the battle of the Herrings, also known as the battle of Rouvray. (It was called the battle of the Herrings because the English used herring barrels to protect themselves.) Joan told the governor the outcome of a battle that had just taken place. No word of the actual event reached him, in fact, for ten days. When it did, Baudricourt must have sent word to Chinon of her presence and her gift of prophecy. As a result, Joan was invited to the court of the dauphin. She did not go at the head of a vast army. Two knights, Jean de Metz and Bertrand de Pouligny, accompanied her, and Joan wore clothing provided for her by the townspeople. Baudricourt, who had given her a sword, watched them depart, saying: "Go! And let come what may!" He had started Joan of Arc on one of the most astounding adventures possible for a human being. She was journeying toward glory, honor, fame, and the horrors of treachery and betrayal.

No one in Domrémy would have recognized Joan, wearing men's clothing, as she rode on horseback toward the city of Chinon. She was dressed as a page, with her hair cut short and topped by a cap. Her short coat served as a tunic, belted at the waist. Underneath she wore a doublet, which was a heavy shirt that was attached to her hose by hooks and leather thongs. She also wore boots, spurs, and a cape.

The eleven-day journey to Chinon was dangerous, as bands of men still roamed the area, looking for gold and jewels. Joan heard her voices throughout, however, and she stopped at Auxerre to hear Mass. Although the townspeople were against the dauphin, they respected Joan's belief that he should be ruler of France. And, so, after her canonization, a statue of Joan was erected in the Auxerre Cathedral, stating that Joan attended Mass there on February 27, 1429.

19

When Joan arrived at Chinon, she was placed in an inn, while the court decided what to do about her and her offer. The royal advisers were fascinated by her and by the possibilities that she offered the dauphin. At the same time, however, many felt that she could be a witch, a heretic — someone who had rejected the Church's teachings — or even a madwoman. It was finally decided to send a committee to meet with her. These men, used to asking questions and making demands of simple people or of those who sought favors from the king, were quite direct in their approach. They asked why she had come to Chinon. Joan explained that God had simply commanded her to break the English siege of the city of Orléans and to bring the dauphin to Reims to be crowned in the traditional fashion.

When the committee reported all this, the court was in an uproar. Some believed she was truly mad, while others argued that she should be given a chance to perform the deeds, just in case this was what God had in mind. The dauphin, still uncertain, sent a group of priests to Joan to study her again. They reported back rather quickly, declaring that there was nothing wrong with her. The priests even recommended that the dauphin meet with her.

Finally, on the night of March 6, 1429, Joan went to the castle of Chinon, where she was escorted into the royal chamber. The courtiers expected her to be dazzled by the luxury, the golden fixtures, and the splendor of the gowns and robes. The dauphin, hoping to trick her, blended into a group of nobles, knowing that this small peasant girl would be too awed to discover him. Joan entered, looked around the room, and went to his side immediately, saying: "I have come, being sent by God, to bring aid to the kingdom and to you."

20

The dauphin, quite shocked at Joan's ability to discover him in the midst of so many finely dressed nobles, appeared to believe her claims and installed her in the tower of the main castle of Chinon. She was placed in the care of a Madame Bellier, the wife of a royal official, who served as an escort and governess. Joan also met the dauphin's cousin, John, duke of Alençon, with whom she would share many battlefield adventures in time.

It was all very rich and glamorous, but the questions and the probes continued along with the feasts and the fancy parties. Joan was sent to the castle at Poitiers, where a new round of interrogations — set patterns of questions and discussions — were begun. Another committee arrived to challenge her word and to decide if she was a witch, as many in the court chose to believe at the time.

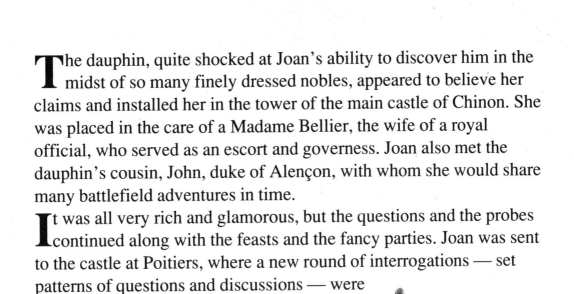

Some of the most learned theologians in France asked about her voices and the task given to her by God. If God wished to deliver France, one asked her, why were soldiers needed at all? She replied that the soldiers would fight and God would grant them a victory. After other talks, the committee told the dauphin to send Joan to Orléans to begin her work there.

21

THE TOWER OF CHINON PALACE

As a result of all of the recommendations, Charles VII gave orders for preparations, declaring Joan the *chef de guerre*, the nation's war chief. He also ordered all of his military officers to follow her commands. By that time, Joan had been joined by two of her brothers, Jean and Pierre. What her father thought of all of this is not known, but he probably allowed his sons to be with her to protect her against harm. The dauphin ordered suits of armor to be made for Joan and her brothers, and armorers from Tours created a special suit of "white" armor for Joan, which gave her a heavenly appearance, even in battle.

Her voices also instructed Joan to put aside the sword that Baudricourt had given her. They told her that the sword she should use would be found at Ste.-Catherine-de-Fierbois, buried near the altar upon which five crosses had been stamped. The astonished priests of the church there were instructed by Joan in a letter and found the sword easily. It was rusted, however, and this alarmed them until they discovered that the rust fell away with a simple wiping. The local weapon masters, paid by the priests, made two sheaths for the sword — the traditional covers — one made out of gold cloth and one out of red velvet. Joan, ever practical, had a leather sheath made for the weapon.

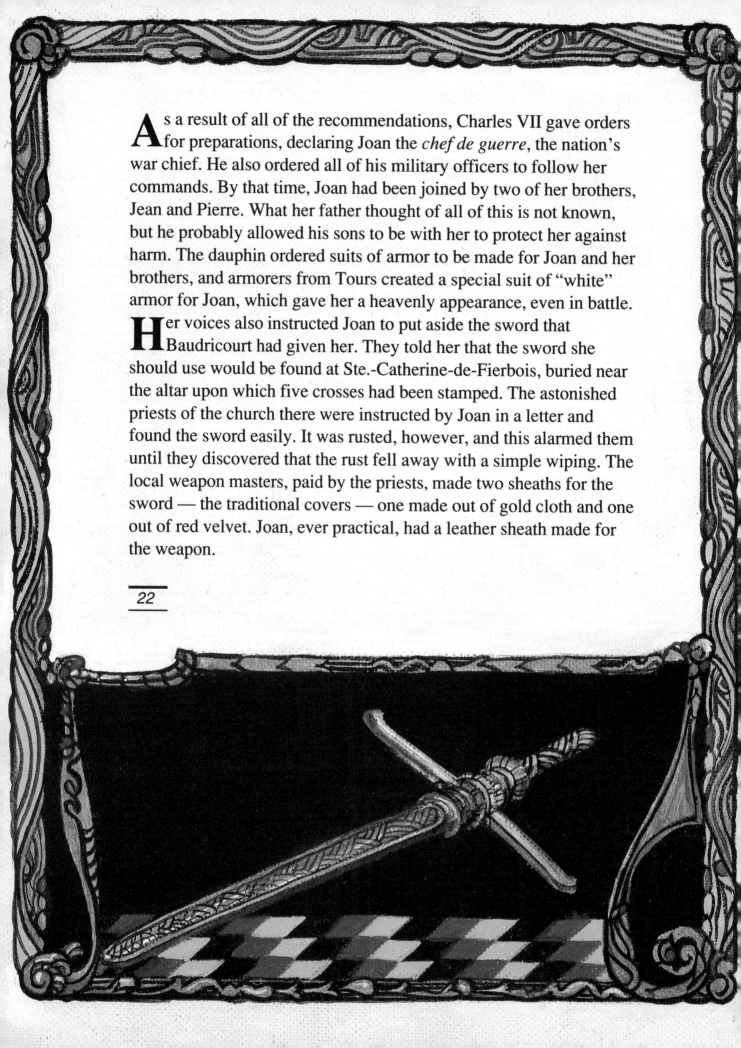

Joan's banner was also an unusual emblem, made of a linenlike material called fustian and trimmed with silk. The decoration was a figure of God, holding the world, with angels kneeling on either side. The words JHESUS (an old way to spell "Jesus") and MARIA were embroidered into it, and the field — the overall area — was decorated with lilies, the symbols of France. A man named Hauves de Poulvoir is said to have made the banner for Joan. His daughter became one of her good friends, and to her Joan confided that the result of her efforts would be wounds and death. When Hauves's daughter asked why Joan would risk such a thing, the Maid of Orléans, as she would soon be called, replied that God had commanded her to do this.

Joan left Tours in late April 1429, going to Blois to join the army there. Reaching the town, she was shocked to see the soldiers drinking and gambling. There were also women in the camp. Joan assembled her officers and instructed them to put a stop to such activities. She also demanded that each soldier make his confession and spend time praying. The soldiers, naturally, laughed when they heard the orders because their way of life was common among armies. They stopped laughing when Joan — banner in hand, mounted on her horse, and escorted by knights — appeared before them. The women, the dice, and the wine were forgotten, and to a man the troops confessed. Prayers echoed throughout the camp in a few days as a clean, sober, and hymn-singing army set out for Orléans. They reached the city in two days and began the relief of Orléans from the English.

23

A rriving at the city (shown above as it appeared in a medieval work), Joan was alarmed by the fact that the army had come to the wrong side of the Loire River. Trusting her generals, especially Dunois, the famed military commander of Orléans, she had allowed her army to be led astray. The entire force would have to cross the water in boats, a reckless and dangerous undertaking. Joan scolded Dunois and others, but they explained that such a position was necessary in order to avoid the local English forts. Miraculously, however, the wind rose, and all of the provisions brought for the city were carried easily across the Loire. While most of the army units moved back to Blois, where there was an easier crossing, Joan entered Orléans on the evening of April 29.

Riding through the gates of Orléans in her white armor, with her banner blowing in the wind, Joan roused the townspeople, who cheered the sight of her. Everyone knew that Orléans would be saved, and as thousands of torchbearers came into the streets to light her parade, the people pushed forward to see and touch her. The champion of France had arrived in their midst.

Settled at last in the city, Joan wrote to Lord John Talbot, the English commander, telling him to withdraw his forces or face disaster. In turn, the English wrote to Joan, announcing that she was just a shepherdess, a simple peasant who should return to her herds before being burned. While these messages were being exchanged, Dunois and other officers went to Blois to lead the French units into the city.

The situation was dangerous, as Joan knew, and she spent time analyzing the military positions. A series of forts on the west were in English hands, and others in the south, called *bastilles*, controlled the south. These were Tourelles and Augustines. Yet another, St. Loup, was located to the east. The English did not have to worry about their northern flank because Paris was in their hands.

On May 4, Dunois and his forces arrived, and there was word that an English relief army was also approaching, led by Sir John Fastolf. (This figure would later appear in Shakespearean plays as Falstaff.) Joan was faced with a decision. She could attack Fastolf or the English forts. Her mind was made up when a French soldier, badly wounded, related how the French were suffering in their assault on the fort of St. Loup.

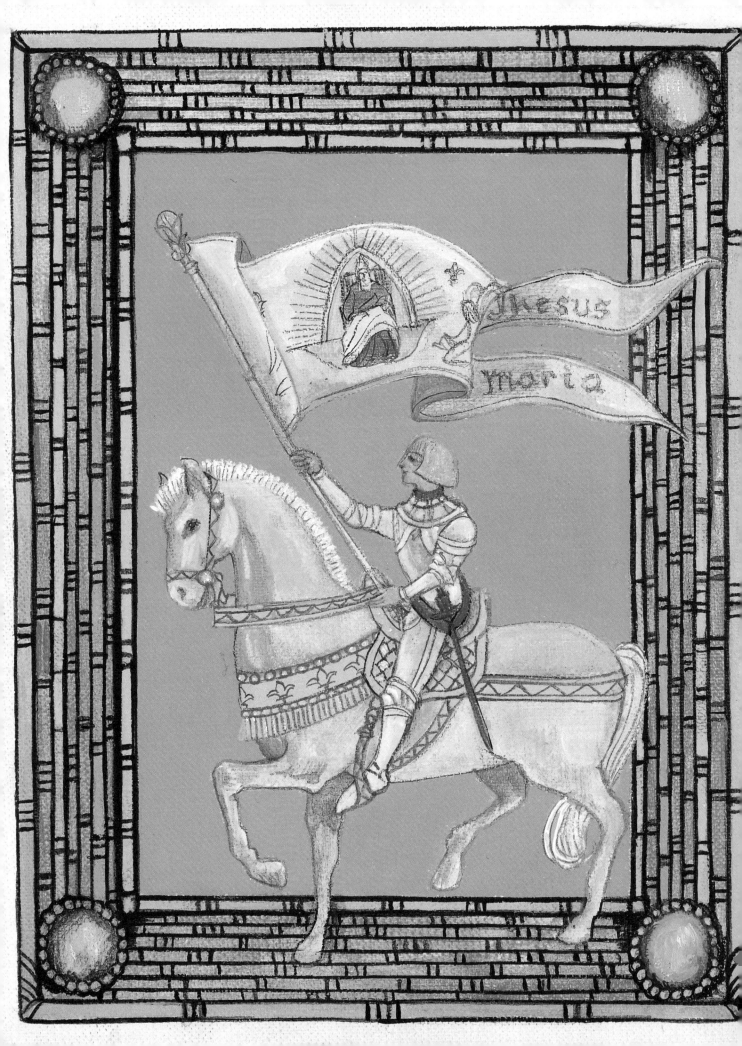

Joan hurried from Orléans, declaring that the war had to be started in earnest. Joined by the bulk of forces in the city, she rode to St. Loup, where the English stared at her with dismay. Despite the fact that they had the upper hand, the sight of her made the English lose heart. Seeing her banner and her white armor glistening in the sun, the English declared that they would not fight a French witch and ran for their lives. The French, delighted by the retreat, swept into St. Loup, and the fortress was theirs.

The voices then commanded Joan to attack Augustines, and once again Joan wrote to the English commander, advising him to leave the scene. She started an assault on May 6, attacking first the little fort to the west of Augustines, St. Jean le Blanc. Troops were ferried across the river again, and Joan joined them in a boat. Those who had gone on ahead were hesitant and afraid until they caught sight of her. The English became afraid at the same image, and they fled to Tourelles.

That night, after giving thanks for another French victory, Joan sat with her commanders, discussing the plans for the next day. She brushed aside their words of restraint and caution, stating that the voices had told her to press on. Joan also predicted that she would be wounded in the next day's battle.

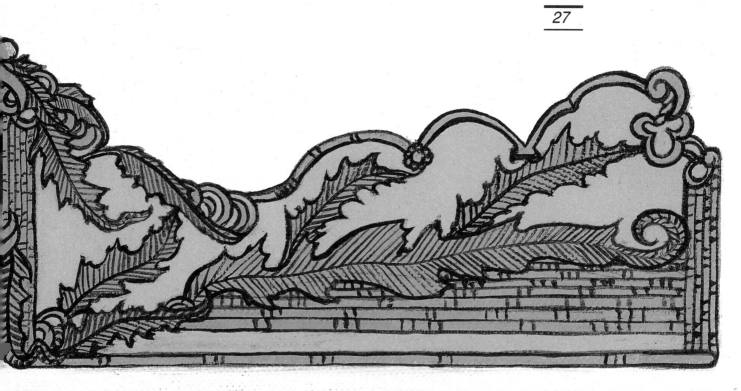

Now, one can imagine how odd it must have been for grim warriors, the commanders of hardened troops, to sit with this young girl, hearing her declare that she would be wounded in the next campaign. The calm with which Joan approached the future, good or bad, is a hallmark — a powerful symbol — of her character. Joan of Arc did not wander about with hymns, prayers, or sermons. She did not join or found a religious order, and she did not display penances in order to bring people to God. Her life was short, painful, and wounded by treachery — the lies and plots — of the very people that she was trying to save. She faced all of these things with resolve, with courage, and with trust in God.

This is the hallmark of her time on earth, her own unique insignia. Once given a command through her voices and visions, Joan did not turn aside, did not complain, and did not try to excuse herself from her duty.

She would be betrayed by those she aided, sold into the hands of the enemy, even tormented by those men who should have honored her voices. In this, Joan of Arc represents another important aspect of human life. She did not expect honors, ranks, rewards, or glory. Joan knew that such things were fleeting. They faded, rusted, and crumbled in time. The human beings who betray others and cheat in order to gain wealth, rank, and fame end up in the same earth as the ones they wounded. Joan understood this well. She knew, as Christ had known in His time in the world, that she would gain nothing but suffering for her deeds at the hands of her fellow human beings. Despite this she obeyed the will of God. For her it was that simple, leaving no room for doubts or excuses.

The following morning, despite warnings and discouraging words from her commanders, Joan gave orders for the attack. The battle raged from morning until late afternoon as men fought on the fields, on walls, and on the barricades. The wounded and dead were piled up on both sides.

Joan, trying to place a ladder against a wall, was struck by a bolt — an arrow — from an enemy crossbow. It pierced her armor in the shoulder near her neck. She fell and was taken from the field. Her armor was removed, and the shaft was taken out of her shoulder. She allowed a dressing made of lard and olive oil to be placed on the wound but then astonished everyone by donning her armor once again and entering the field.

The English troops, discovering Joan in the battle again, felt panic in their ranks. She had appeared mortally wounded, and now she was whole and powerful again. Her banner shone, and her armor glistened in the sun as she urged her men forward. It was too much! The English fled the scene. Meanwhile, the French, taking advantage of the panic, sailed a burning boat up the river and set fire to the wooden drawbridge, which was the only route of escape from Tourelles. When it collapsed, a large part of the English forces was captured.

29

DUNOIS OF ORLÉANS

L ord Glasdale, the military commander of the fort, drowned along with many English nobles as a result of the fire. Those who did survive were captured by the French who had managed to cross the river unseen. The English not only surrendered but retreated from their forts around Orléans. Joan of Arc did not give orders to pursue them, however, as Sunday morning dawned. She said that the duty of the army was to attend Mass and to give thanks.

W ord of the campaign and the retreat of the English spread like wildfire across the land, and a miraculous response took place in villages, towns, and cities. Joan was the champion of France. She was the savior of the nation, which meant the victor of a united people. Those living in the region suddenly realized that they were truly one. Rich or poor, powerful or lowly, the people united and began to think of themselves as French.

J oan, preparing to appear before the dauphin in order to report her victories, received word that Charles VII was on his way to Tours. She rode there, banner in hand, bowing low before him when they met. Together, the Maid of Orléans and the dauphin entered Tours, where the people went mad with joy. Joan was called *La Pucelle* ("The Maid") by the French, and the sight of her cheered everyone.

A fter the first festivities, Joan asked the dauphin to go to Reims to be crowned, but his advisers stated their doubts. Several cities on the way to Reims were still in English hands, they claimed, and Charles would be placed in danger. As usual, Charles did not argue with his courtiers and appeared nervous and afraid.

Taking time to listen to her voices, Joan then volunteered to clear the entire Loire Valley of English troops. Money was found easily because of Joan's fame, and a new army was formed. Joan probably had from five thousand to six thousand Frenchmen under her command at the time. The army also had siege machines and supplies.

They faced the English armies of Lord John Talbot and Sir John Fastolf, as well as the English garrisons along the road to Reims. Joan set the first objective as Jargeau, just north of Orléans. It was commanded by two brothers, John and Alexander de la Pole, under the overall authority of their brother, the duke of Suffolk. These two men were able to repel Joan's first attack on their fort, but Joan stood before the French troops, holding her standard and urging them to "have a good heart!"

By nightfall the English were entirely enclosed within their fortress in Jargeau. Joan sent them a warning, as she always did in battles, telling them that they would be attacked the following morning. Her message lowered the morale of the English troops who believed she would put a terrible spell on them all. So powerful was her image that the English did not even dare to attack the French positions during the night, although Joan had set no guards. The French rested and prepared, and the English waited and turned to other ways of bringing down the Maid of Orléans — methods that were cruel and leading ultimately to her martyrdom.

31

The next morning the attack began with the French guns opening up on the walls of Jargeau. When the English returned the fire, Joan called out to her trusted lieutenant, the duke of Alençon, who was a cousin of the dauphin. She warned the duke that he had to move from his place or be killed by cannon fire. He took her advice and walked some distance away. A man who went to stand in his original place was killed there just moments later. Joan, it seems, had promised Alençon's wife that she would bring him safely home from the campaign, and she did.

Leading the charge against the walls of the city, Joan was struck by a rock and fell from the ladder she was climbing. To the shock and horror of the English, she stood up immediately and began to lead the attack again. The equally stunned French rallied around her, and Jargeau fell into their hands. Among the English prisoners taken were the duke of Suffolk, the area English commander, John de la Pole.

Other forts and other towns surrendered after the defeat of Jargeau, and in a short time the French were able to sweep into the Loire Valley. The English were bringing up a relief army to aid in their defense, but the English soldiers were unhappy about facing the "witch," as they called Joan. During the night, in fact, these units retreated.

32

Joan and the French gave chase, and when they caught up with the English the battle of Patay started. The enemy tried hard to outrun the French, not wanting to make their men face someone they feared so greatly. Their supply wagons and the size of their units worked against them, however, and eventually they had to turn, regroup, and take a stand.

The battle of Patay started with a strange omen that made the English even more afraid. A stag appeared at the edge of a clearing, just in front of the advance English units. When they caught sight of the magnificent animal, they forgot about the battle and the dangers and started to yell and chase the stag. The French commander, a man named Étienne de Vignoles, also called La Hire, took advantage of the situation instantly and crashed into the disorganized ranks of the enemy. The English archers, feared by armies all across Europe, were slain before they could shoot their arrows, and Fastolf, the commander, raced from the scene. He was headed back to the main defenses in order to strengthen them against attack, but his own troops, seeing him, believed he was fleeing from Joan the "witch." They broke ranks and ran as fast as they could. Soon the entire army was in flight. Many died in a terrible slaughter, and Joan comforted one English soldier who died in her arms.

33

THE DUKE OFALENÇON

Once again the Maid of Orléans was victorious, and the English wanted nothing to do with her or her armies. The towns in the region who had supported the English were also having second thoughts about the situation. Their alliances with the enemy were proving liabilities, something they would have to answer for in the growing sense of French nationalism.

Actually, the battle of Patay is considered to be the crowning achievement of Joan's brief military career. She seemed to have a remarkable sense of military strategy, and she dared to take risks with herself and her men in order to cleanse the land of enemy stain. Because of Orléans, Jargeau, and now Patay, the Loire Valley lay open before the French. The English were forced to withdraw to Paris to regroup and to come up with a plan to stop this young warrior woman. The English had lost an entire army at Orléans, as well as many of their best commanders. Patay, however, wounded their cause even more. There Joan seemed enveloped in the protection of God, invulnerable to English attacks. Also, as a result, the French were uniting once again.

Most importantly, Reims was now open. The dauphin could be crowned in the cathedral there, taking the legitimate titles that would be the undoing of English plans.

34

Now, while everyone else, including the English, could see how Joan's triumphs had placed the dauphin in a true position of power, Charles VII was not so sure. Giving in to his normal nervousness, and listening to his advisers, who were sick to death of Joan and her wars, he began to grumble about the dangers still present. Some of the towns on the way to Reims were allies of the English. Joan urged the dauphin to start out for Reims, declaring that she and the French army would take on the renegade towns. She captured Auxerre and St. Florentine rather quickly and then faced the city of Troyes.

As usual, Joan wrote to the city fathers of Troyes, telling them to surrender or face disaster. Her letters, which she dictated to scribes, have been saved over the centuries, and they are quite astonishing. Joan was very literate, used excellent French, and spoke with command and with authority. In other words, these were not the letters of some country bumpkin.

The city fathers of Troyes did not submit just because of a letter, however, and this reaction brought the dauphin into another nervous fit. A council was gathered to discuss the situation. Joan of Arc was not invited to the council until a senior member of the court demanded her presence. Once seated with the dauphin and his nervous friends, however, she calmly announced that Troyes would fall within two days. The way in which she said this, with confidence and no hesitation on her part, so startled Charles VII that he took hold of himself and gave permission to Joan and Alençon to start the attack.

Now, it is difficult to picture this young woman in the presence of nobles, military officials, courtiers, and the dauphin. Most young women of her historical period would have fainted or ran at the sight of such powerful men. Joan entered their courts, heard their complaints and their fears, and then counseled them to courage. She was not born a warrior, did not come from a long line of warriors. None of this came to her as part of her inheritance. God alone had provided the grace, the courage, and the really remarkable wisdom that Joan displayed on all occasions during her military career.

It is important to remember this because the person known as Joan of Arc can be lost in the battles, in the wars, and in the opulent ceremonies of the courts. She was a peasant woman, from a small town, in a rather quiet region of France, but God had placed her in the whirlpool — in the churning, spinning center of activity — just to offer France and its nervous monarch salvation and victory.

Back in Troyes, meanwhile, the city fathers were becoming a bit nervous themselves. It is one thing to laugh in the face of the enemy but quite another to make war on your own countrymen for the sake of an invading foe. The tales of Joan's victories began to trickle into Troyes, and the city fathers were entertaining second thoughts about the entire affair. They decided to send out a delegation to speak with the Maid of Orléans, headed by a priest called Brother Richard.

It is hard to tell whether Brother Richard was just naturally anxious about things in life or filled with stories that were running across France about the Maid. When Joan came up to meet with the priest and his fellow delegates, he made the sign of the cross. Perhaps he expected a bolt of lightning to crash out of the sky, devouring Joan. Perhaps he thought the ground would open up and swallow her whole. Just to be really safe, Brother Richard also sprinkled her with holy water. She certainly would shriek in pain or vanish in a cloud of smoke with such blessed drops on her skin.

To Brother Richard's astonishment, Joan of Arc laughed at his precautions. "Approach, I will not fly away," she said, and the delegation drew near. Actually, after the surrender, which Brother Richard and his fellow townsmen rather easily arranged, the priest attached himself to Joan's staff. He remained faithful to her because he saw that she was a woman who could laugh and be amused by the responses of others. This was no "witch," and this was no angry weapon of God. Joan was a young woman, made of flesh and blood like the rest of us, capable of being hurt or angry. The one thing that made her stand out from most people was her total surrender to the will of God.

Upon hearing of the surrender of Troyes, as Joan had predicted, the dauphin and his courtiers went to the city. Part of the surrender terms allowed for the retreat of the English and Burgundian troops. They were more than delighted to be away from the "witch." They exited from Troyes but took French prisoners with them. Joan bargained for the release of her countrymen, and the dauphin paid their ransoms.

Two days later, after the surrender of Troyes and another town, Châlons, the dauphin and his court reached the city of Reims. Long loyal to the royal cause, the people of Reims cheered as Charles VII and Joan entered the gates. Charles's coronation was set for July 17, 1429, a rather hurried date but decided upon because Reims could not house the court and the army for long. The people managed to decorate every street and corner overnight for the occasion.

Following the ancient traditions, the coronation was preceded by a group of fully armed knights, who brought back the ampule (or vial) of holy oils, believed to have descended from heaven centuries ago and kept safe in the abbey church of St. Remy. The knights returned to the cathedral of Reims and rode their horses into the building, followed by the king and his grand procession. Alençon knighted Charles VII to make him worthy of the throne, and then the archbishop of Reims consecrated him. The entire service lasted from nine in the morning until two in the afternoon. Shouts of *Noël!* echoed in the cathedral when the anointing of the king took place and when the crown was put upon his head. Trumpets blared so often and so loud that some attending the ceremony said that they thought the walls of the cathedral were going to come crashing down.

Joan was present, standing in her white armor, with her banner in hand. When Charles was crowned, she bowed low before him, saying: "Good King, now is fulfilled the will of God that the siege of Orléans be raised and that you be brought to Reims to be crowned to show that you are the true king and that the kingdom of France belongs to you."

Joan's brothers were with her at the ceremony, and her father, Jacques, was present also. He had walked from Domrémy to Reims in order to share in his daughter's triumph. Jacques received a purse of gold from the king, and his hotel bill was paid by the city fathers. He did not walk home to Domrémy but rode a fine horse, another gift.

When asked what Joan desired as her reward, she stated that she would like to see the suffering of the people in the villages of Domrémy and Greux eased by a lessening of their taxes. Charles VII signed a decree making that possible, and in the tax records of France from that day forward the names of the towns of Domrémy and Greux were listed with the phrase *Neant, la Pucelle* ("Nothing, the Maid"). This tax-free status continued for over three hundred years, ending with the French Revolution.

Also present at the coronation were the two knights who had escorted the Maid of Orléans to Chinon: Jean de Metz and Bertrand de Poulegny. Her "uncle" Durand Laxart received notice at the ceremonies also.

The bells, the shouts of the people, and the joy echoing through the streets echoed again and again throughout France as the nation awakened slowly to its own destiny and to its sense of being unified under the rightful king.

As happy as the celebrations were for all concerned, for Joan of Arc the days in Reims marked the high point of her career. From this occasion on, in fact, forces would meet with only one purpose: to destroy the Maid and her hold on France. The English were not jumping up and down with happiness over the coronation, and the Burgundians — always scheming to take the throne from Charles VII and his family — began to send their spies and agents into the countryside. A promise was made here, a bribe was paid there, and soon greedy men and those with ambitions were working to see Joan dead.

The king's court was filled with people who looked forward to the same thing. Charles himself probably resented the way Joan had pushed him to the heights of greatness. Now that he sat on the throne of France, no matter how shaky it was in truth, he saw no reason for keeping her as his champion. In fact, her presence actually made matters worse politically. No court in Europe at the time could stand up to the simple demands of a pure, unwavering woman of God like Joan.

Perhaps she always understood the dangers around her. Asked what she feared most in the world, Joan always replied: "Treachery." She had a great deal to fear from the English and the Burgundians. Joan also faced genuine danger from the court of Charles VII. The forces were gathering, the skies darkening, and the Maid of Orléans was about to face the one thing in the world that she feared. This treachery would be made crueler because it would come from the very people who should have moved to help her.

When the last trumpet had sounded and the last *Noël!* had faded into the glare of the sun, Joan realized that there was still much to be accomplished. She said good-bye to her father and then started planning an assault on the city of Paris. The English and the Burgundians still ruled there, and a sudden and swift campaign could have taken them by surprise. Joan proposed such a move to Charles. Paris was only three days away, and the enemy was disorganized and wounded by the coronation and the taste of bitter defeats at her hands. The courtiers and advisers, however, were not particularly anxious to see Paris set free, especially if Joan of Arc was to get credit for the act. One courtier, in fact, hatched a plot with the archbishop of Reims, the very man who had crowned the king in the cathedral. These two met secretly with agents of Philip, duke of Burgundy.

Their reasons for plotting against Joan and the king were quite simple: greed and ambition. Both the courtier and the archbishop had become wealthy because of the war. They had trade interests everywhere, sold goods to the English, and took what they could from the poor people.

If Joan and her army took the city of Paris, many of their markets would be closed, and the English and the Burgundians would not be so willing to do business. These men, traitors to the king and to France, were desperate at the thought of the Maid winning another victory.

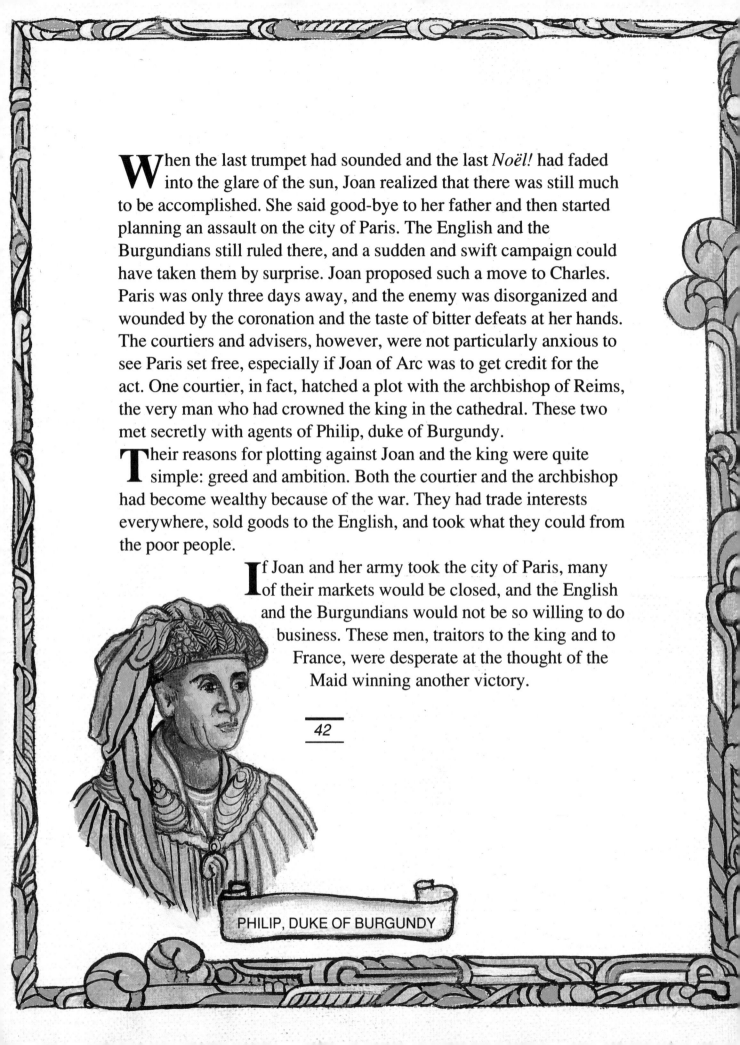

PHILIP, DUKE OF BURGUNDY

Now, it comes as a shock to hear about bishops and courtiers plotting against their king and country, but each age of the world has its own kind of treachery and ugliness. The archbishop of Reims was greedy and eager to live the good life, and he didn't care about France or the weak man on the throne of the land. He and others began to talk Charles VII into making a truce with the Burgundians, knowing that the king was weak enough to hope that he could avoid war. The Burgundians played the same game, offering to sign a treaty in Paris within a few months if Charles stopped Joan and her army.

Charles, naturally, wanted to win Paris without much effort, and he stopped all talk of a campaign to free Paris. He was not even upset when he heard that the English were bringing large armies into the city. A treaty was actually signed on August 1, and the Burgundians promised to surrender Paris by the middle of that month. Joan and others knew that it was a trick. The treaty wasn't worth the paper it was written on. Charles refused their arguments, and he stopped all talk about Paris and campaigns.

Eventually, however, Joan led an army toward Paris, as even Charles realized that the English and the Burgundians were not going to hand over Paris without a fight. Joan met the forces of the English near the town of Senlis. Not eager to face Joan in an open battle, the duke of Bedford, the English commander, took up defensive positions. No matter how many times they were challenged, the English did not come out, and eventually, under cover of darkness, they would sneak away, moving toward Paris.

In the court, meanwhile, people were telling the king that Joan's love of war had brought about the latest problems. Her rash and reckless advances had caused the Burgundians to deny the treaty. Charles was residing in Compiègne at the time, one of the towns that had surrendered to him in the face of the English retreat. A Burgundian bishop, a man named Pierre Cauchon, had been forced to flee as a result. The idea of having to leave his comforts so enraged this bishop that Cauchon swore vengeance upon Joan of Arc. Unfortunately for the Maid, Cauchon was one of those terrible individuals who worked tirelessly to carry out his threats.

Joan had decided to march on Paris, something which so alarmed the English and the Burgundians that they offered Charles a new treaty. By the terms of this pact, Joan could have Paris, but the English and the Burgundians would claim all of northern France. Charles, probably in a state of confusion and exhaustion, offered the enemy the city of Compiègne as part of the deal. This did not sit well with the people of that city, however, and they raced out into the streets to shout their defiance of both Charles and the English, and he abandoned the idea as he abandoned everything else if he had to fight for it.

Joan's voices had not ordered her to attack Paris. She had started the campaign because she believed it necessary, but her voices and her visions had not commanded her to make that move.

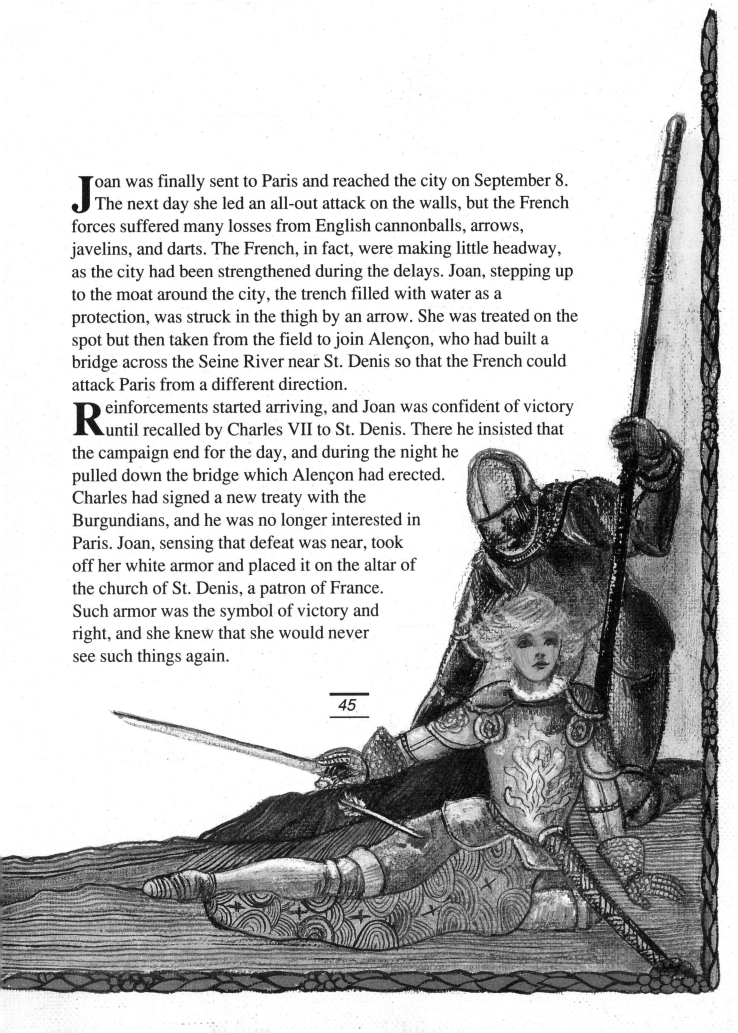

Joan was finally sent to Paris and reached the city on September 8. The next day she led an all-out attack on the walls, but the French forces suffered many losses from English cannonballs, arrows, javelins, and darts. The French, in fact, were making little headway, as the city had been strengthened during the delays. Joan, stepping up to the moat around the city, the trench filled with water as a protection, was struck in the thigh by an arrow. She was treated on the spot but then taken from the field to join Alençon, who had built a bridge across the Seine River near St. Denis so that the French could attack Paris from a different direction.

Reinforcements started arriving, and Joan was confident of victory until recalled by Charles VII to St. Denis. There he insisted that the campaign end for the day, and during the night he pulled down the bridge which Alençon had erected. Charles had signed a new treaty with the Burgundians, and he was no longer interested in Paris. Joan, sensing that defeat was near, took off her white armor and placed it on the altar of the church of St. Denis, a patron of France. Such armor was the symbol of victory and right, and she knew that she would never see such things again.

45

Kept inactive and surrounded by the luxuries and the pleasures of the court, Joan and her family were ennobled by Charles VII. They were given the name Du Lys with noble ranks. If this was supposed to appease Joan, to make her accept the endless court entertainments, luxuries, and wastes, it did not work. When a letter came from Reims, declaring that the city was about to be attacked by the English, Joan wrote encouraging letters and then begged permission to attack the enemy again.

Unpopular in the court, Joan and her trusted lieutenants were not able to raise funds or troops. In late March of 1430, Joan and her comrades-in-arms left Sully, where the court was in sessions. Only a few in number originally, their appearance attracted vast crowds, and an army was being mobilized once again against the English and their Burgundian allies.

After the campaigns, Joan then heard from her voices that she would be captured and that she should accept all things as the will of God. She would die not in battle, as she had hoped; instead she would fall into the hands of her vicious enemies. The French people of the region did not seem particularly good allies either. Soissons and other towns refused to send food or men and even shut their city gates in Joan's face. In time the units that she had drawn to the cause melted away, as the men realized the cause was becoming hopeless.

At Compiègne, the last battle in which Joan took part, she wore simple armor and a crimson cloak embroidered in gold. There she surprised the Burgundians who were guarding a bridge and might have won the day if a nearby English commander had not sent immediate reinforcements. The French were outnumbered quickly, but Joan pressed on the attack. Despite warnings from her comrades, she continued until the governor of Compiègne, a man named De Flavy, became afraid that the enemy would enter the city and raised the drawbridge. This left Joan defenseless on the bank of the river.

An archer in the ranks of the Burgundian commander, John of Luxembourg, dragged Joan from her horse and made her a prisoner. She and her aides were taken to Luxembourg's tent, where she was put on display for the English and the Burgundians. When John, duke of Bedford, the supreme commander of the English forces, realized that they had the Maid, he started a plot to kill her.

Bedford, however, decided that it was better if the Church officials carried out the murder themselves. He knew that men like Bishop Cauchon and theologians from the University of Paris could be counted upon to stain their hands with Joan's blood for the sake of vengeance. The Maid of Orléans had inconvenienced them all in the past. Using such men, Bedford could slay (that is, kill) Joan and strengthen the cause of England's new king, Henry VI. Henry V had died in 1422.

Joan was not going to sit idle in captivity, however, and she tried to escape almost immediately. She was moved to a more distant place, and there she tried again to escape and fell into a moat. The English found her there, unconscious. Such courage made Bedford uneasy, and through Bishop Cauchon he arranged to buy Joan from Philip the Good of Burgundy. This duke was actually called Good by his people because they approved of what he was doing. Selling Joan of Arc to her enemies was a political move, worthy of praise by the Burgundians.

47

Thus began months of agony for Joan, as she fell victim to cruel men on January 3, 1431. Her judges were Bishop Pierre Cauchon and a man named Jean Lemaitre. Their purpose was to make the entire farce — the ridiculous, insane mockery of truth — look legal. Joan was held in Bouvreuil Castle, chained twenty-four hours a day to a block of wood. Her guards insulted her and laughed at her, and others, including King Henry VI of England, visited her to make fun of her condition. Her cell was cold and windowless.

After weeks of questions and sermons, Joan's trial started officially on March 24, 1431, with seventy separate charges read against her. All of them were odd, including one about her use of male clothing, and another which attacked the fact that the voices spoke to her in French. The judges apparently felt that saints and angels only spoke English. If the voices had talked in English, Joan, of course, would not have understood a word. These and other peculiar charges were eventually reduced to twelve, all designed to label her a witch. She collapsed as a result of her treatment and became seriously ill.

Not wanting Joan to die in their care, the judges had her nursed back to health. They threatened her with torture while she was recovering, and the judges even took a vote on the use of torture. Two supported the use of fire and hideous machines, but ten opposed such cruelty.

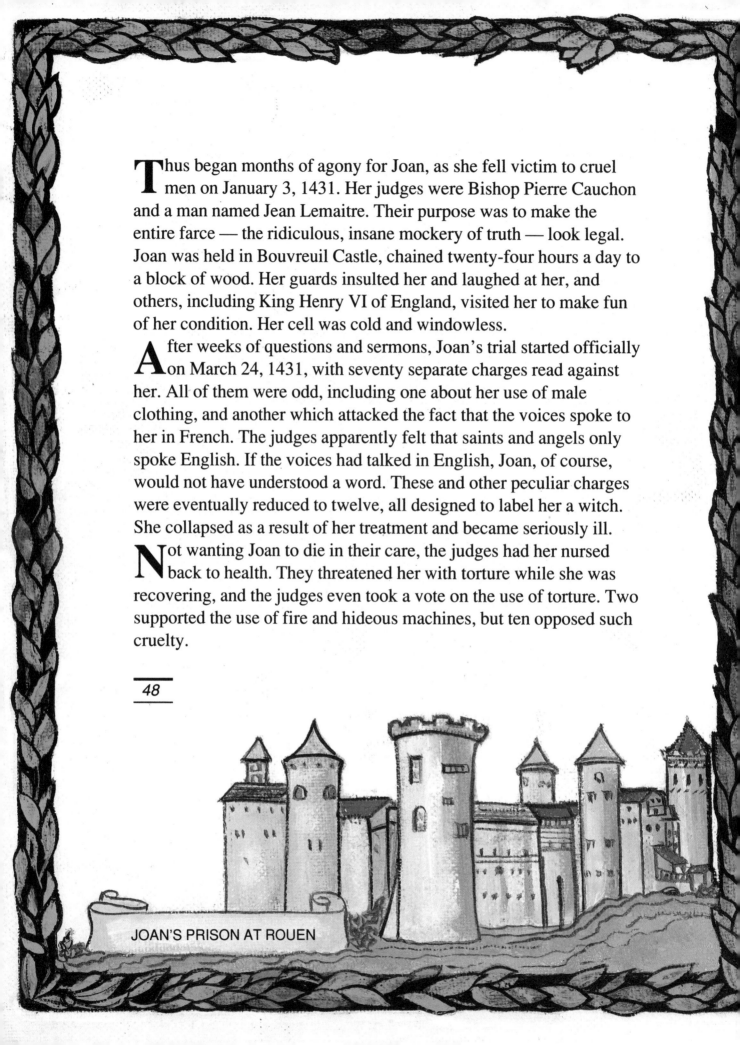

JOAN'S PRISON AT ROUEN

On May 23, Joan was told that she would be handed over to the state officials for execution. She finally agreed, out of exhaustion and hopelessness, to deny that her voices were from God. Forced to wear women's clothing, Joan soon discovered that her jailers had stolen her skirts and blouses. They left behind a suit of men's clothes, and she was forced to put on those garments. The English, delighted that she had fallen into their trap, declared that she had once again taken up her old ways of witchcraft and heresy. The male clothing was a sign, they announced.

Joan, in turn, faced her enemies with a sudden fierce power that made them uneasy. She informed them that her voices had scolded her for denying them, and that she would die before she would give in again. Torture, death by flames, anything that the English and the Burgundians could hand out would be better than admitting to lies. The evil ambitions of Cauchon and his plotters would never again turn her aside from her duty. Struck by her anger, the judges signed the death warrant of Joan of Arc.

She had taken the worst that they could give her, and she had triumphed, as anyone who suffers innocently or at the hands of evil men wins out in the end. Joan weighed heaven against their threats and their promises, and she accepted the will of God. He alone allowed such men to live and to prosper. He alone would bring her to His side. The men might plot and take their revenge, but death awaited them too in time, and the grave would not hide their evil.

49

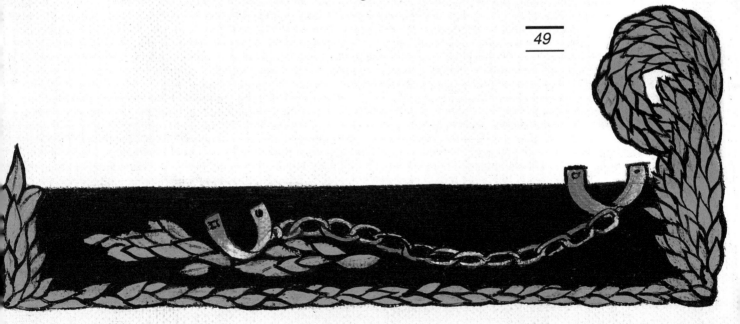

On the morning of May 30, 1431, Joan was granted the right to make her last confession by Pierre Cauchon. This did not make any sense at all! If Joan was a witch and a heretic, why would she want to go to confession? Why would a court that had condemned her as a witch and a heretic allow her to make such a confession? Joan also received Holy Communion, which would never have been given to a "witch" who traded in lies and magic.

After she was led to the Place du Vieux-Marché, where she heard one last sermon, Joan was tied to a stake and her sentence was read aloud. As the men piled wood around her and lighted the flames, a Dominican priest held up a crucifix so that she could end her life with this vision before her. The priest shouted through the flames and the smoke that she would soon be in paradise.

As the flames began to blister her flesh, and as her small body slowly disappeared in the fire and billows of dark smoke, the men who had plotted her death found little joy in it. One English soldier who had been waiting to put a log on her death pyre — the mound of wood and flames — turned away in horror as he was convinced that he saw Joan's soul rise out of the flames in the form of a white dove. The learned judges took to their beds in remorse, and others fled the scene with dread. The executioner said later that Joan's heart had not burned in the fire but was intact when the ashes were removed.

51

Throughout France a silent moan emerged from the lips of the people when word came of her execution by fire. Many of her comrades-in-arms had probably believed that she would be ransomed by the king. The simple people turned from their leaders in disgust and horror, knowing that the Maid of Orléans had been sacrificed for the greed and ambitions of men.

Pierre Cauchon, having achieved the act of vengeance against Joan, was shunned by his fellow human beings for the rest of his life. He did not become an archbishop and died quite suddenly eleven years after Joan's death. He was later found guilty of many scandals, and his body was removed from its elaborate tomb and thrown into a ditch. Others involved in the trial and execution died or fell from grace quickly. One, Nicholas Midi, became a leper — a fact which impressed the French people.

The English cause failed when John, duke of Bedford, died, and even the dukes of Burgundy saw the eventual collapse of their own powers and ranks. Paris fell in 1436, and then Normandy and other territories were taken back by the French. In 1453, Bordeaux, the last city captured by the English outside of Calais, surrendered to the forces of Charles VII. The English, caught up in the terrible War of the Roses, were never able to recover their military might, due mainly to the efforts of the Maid.

52

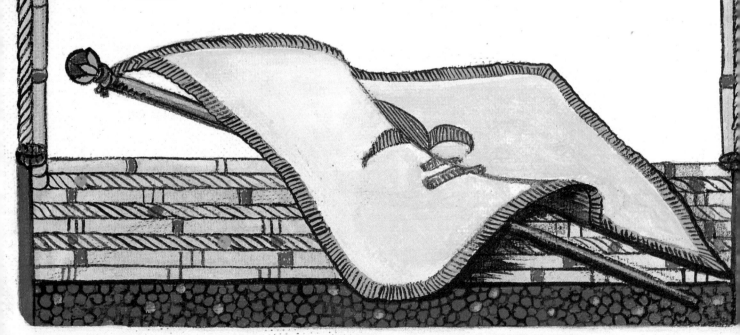

Charles VII, who appeared to have forgotten Joan of Arc entirely, decided after twenty years to rehabilitate her memory — in other words, to undo the damage to her name and reputation. The charges made against her, that of witchcraft and heresy, remained like shadows over him. The English and others could laugh and say that he had to employ a "witch" to gain his throne. A trial was thus opened in 1450, lasting for six years and ending in Rouen.

Joan's name was cleared by the testimony of her mother and her comrades-in-arms. Joan's father had died soon after her martyrdom, probably of a broken heart. The Church also became involved, and Cardinal d'Estouteville, the bishop of Digne, and Jean Brehal, the inquisitor of France, were empowered to make their own investigations. The cardinal declared that the entire trial was irregular. Nothing came of the investigation or its decisions, however, until June 11, 1455, when Pope Calixtus III, a member of the Borgia family, instituted a new investigation. While few of the actual judges and tormentors were named, and while the English were not singled out, the outcome of this new investigation was the same as the first. In Notre Dame Church in Paris the decision was read aloud. Joan was declared innocent of all charges, and her trial was censured, along with the individuals involved.

Now, all these legal acts only confirmed what the people of Europe at the time already knew. The various reasons for the illegality of the trial had already been discussed by the simple people, who did not need the fancy writings or the endless testimony of witnesses to prove the case. The English

ST. JOAN OF ARC

had corrupted the Church courts for their own ends and had used ambitious, greedy men to slay the Maid. The reasons for their corruption and murderous intentions were quite plain. If Joan had heard voices telling her to save the king and to rid the land of the English, then the English and the Burgundians were the enemies of what was right and good. If God had raised up a young girl to stop the best laid plans of the English, then these plans violated His will. Political skills, treaties, alliances, even wars — none of these things could erase this simple fact. Joan of Arc was the symbol of God's intentions for France. The announcement made in July 1456 used fancy phrases, naming "certain enemies" as evil, but the people of Europe could read between the lines.

For the loyal supporters of Joan of Arc the announcement was hard-won and long overdue. Isabelle, her mother, was granted a pension by the city of Orléans and died there in 1458. She had titles and ranks by that time, as the entire family was given such honors by the king. Joan's brother took the place of the governor who had aided Joan in the beginning of her public life, becoming Baudricourt's successor. Durand Laxart, her "uncle," lived for many years and was honored as Joan's friend. Pierre, her older brother, remained in Orléans, also on a pension. The family was known by that time as the noble Du Lys.

Charles VII, ever strange, ever stingy with his gratitude and praise, ruled until 1461, but his reign was not a happy one. He rebuilt France and proved an able king, but he was also plagued with problems and died unloved by his family and people.

In 1904, the cause of Joan of Arc was officially opened, as veneration for her had increased during the five hundred years following her murder at the stake. Declared venerable — the first title given to any candidate for sainthood after being deemed worthy of honors — Joan was praised in plays, literary works, and in various paintings.

In 1909, Joan of Arc was beatified, the second stage in the canonization process, the second phase of bringing to the world the life and virtues of an individual. On May 16, 1920, in St. Peter's in Rome, Joan of Arc was canonized, declared a true saint of the Church. The Maid of Orléans had long been a patron of France, but now her story spread across the earth, and millions of human beings heard about this gallant young woman who dared everything for the will of God.